# *Meeting*

# of

# Minds

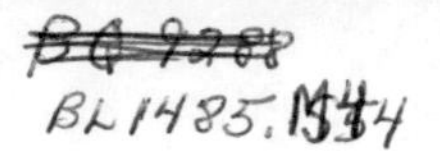


# *Meeting*

# of

# Minds

## A Dialogue on Tibetan and Chinese Buddhism

H. H. the 14th Dalai Lama

Venerable Chan Master Sheng-yen

Dharma Drum Publications • New York

Dharma Drum Publications
90-56 Corona Avenue
Elmhurst, New York 11373
United States of America

Tel: 718/595-0915
Fax: 718-592-0717
Email: dharmadrm@aol.com

To promote wisdom and compassion in our world, Dharma Drum Publications is delighted to make this and other booklets available for free distribution around the world. Our ability to publish and distribute booklets such as this depends solely upon your kindness and assistance. Donations—tax deductible in the USA—may be sent to Dharma Drum Publications at the above address, and we thank most sincerely the sponsors of this and other booklets we have produced in the past. Please let us know if you would like to join us in spreading the teaching of wisdom and compassion to all people everywhere.

ISBN 1-890684-03-1



FOR FREE DISTRIBUTION

Printed in the United States of America on recycled paper

# Acknowledgments

Translators: Wang Ming Yee, Geshe Thubten Jinpa, Guo-gu Bhikshu
Editor: Lindley Hanlon and Ernest Heau
Editorial Assistance: Guo-gu Bhikshu, Alex Wang, and John Anello
Production: Guo-gu Bhikshu
Cover Design: Guo-gu Bhikshu and Chih-ching Lee
Cover Photos: Guo-gu Bhikshu (New York City scene); Kevin Hsieh
(H. H. the Dalai Lama and Venerable Sheng-yen)
Photos that appear in the book: Kevin Hsieh

Dharma Drum Publications gratefully acknowledges all those who generously contributed to the publication and distribution of this book.

# CONTENTS

# FOREWORD

On May 1st through the 3rd, 1998, His Holiness the 14th Dalai Lama and Venerable Chan Master Sheng-yen presented *In the Spirit of Manjushri: the Wisdom Teachings of Buddhism*, at the Roseland in New York City. Tibet House New York and the Dharma Drum Mountain Buddhist Association sponsored the event, which drew some 2500 people from all Buddhist traditions, as well as scholars of medicine, comparative religion, psychology, education, and comparative religion from around the world. It was a three-day discourse designed to promote understanding among Chinese, Tibetan, and Western Buddhists. His Holiness presented two and a half days of teaching on Tibetan Buddhism. A dialogue with Venerable Master Sheng-yen, one of the foremost scholars and teachers of Chinese Chan [Zen] Buddhism, followed on the afternoon of the third day. This book is the result of that dialogue.

That auspicious occasion was the first time that His Holiness and Venerable Sheng-yen engaged in a formal Buddhist discussion, although they had met before on several occasions.

His Holiness and Venerable Sheng-yen discussed topics on the transformation of mind. Much of their dialogue focused on the connection between *kleshas* [mental afflictions], meditation practice, and the experience of enlightenment.

The "sudden" and "gradual" approaches to enlightenment was an important topic. This issue was once debated by the Indian master Kamalashila and the Chinese master Hoshang, around 792 in Tibet. His Holiness and Venerable Sheng-yen made it clear that there is no real contradiction between the sudden and gradual approaches. The differences lie in the dispositions of the practitioners.

His Holiness and Venerable Sheng-yen also clarified some common misconceptions held by the Chinese and Tibetan traditions. Chinese Buddhists often believe that Tibetan Buddhism emphasizes "esotericism," and Tibetan Buddhists often believe that theirs is the most "complete" Buddhist teaching.

While it is true that Tibetan Buddhism absorbed some non-Buddhist tantric approaches to practice, nevertheless, it remains grounded in the Four Noble Truths, especially the truth of cessation of suffering, or emptiness, which is one of the most important characteristics of correct Dharma.

Although Chinese Buddhism did not incorporate translations of late Indian Buddhist scriptures, it nevertheless continued the teachings on emptiness in a dynamic way, which eventually flowered into Chan Buddhism. According to historians, Chan also had an important impact on the meditative traditions of Tibetan Buddhism.

This dialogue between two Buddhist masters symbolizes the commonality between all Buddhist paths of awakening, and it celebrates the meeting of two great minds. We hope that their meeting and this book will initiate further exchange and cooperation between these two great traditions.

When there is unity among Buddhists, Buddhadharma flourishes, which can further peace and harmony throughout the world. As Venerable Sheng-yen often says, "We can build a Pure Land in this world."

We are grateful to His Holiness for his permission to reprint sections of *An Introduction to Buddhism and Tantric Meditation* from Paljor Publications, which supplements the first part of this book. We are also grateful to Venerable Chan Master Sheng-yen for initializing this project and his keen interest in establishing exchange programs between Tibetan and Chinese Buddhist studies.

We are also grateful to Robert and Nena Thurman and their staff at Tibet House, for cosponsoring *In the Spirit of Manjushri: the Wisdom Teachings of Buddhism.*

I would like to extend my heartfelt thanks to the many other bodhisattvas that helped create this event and the resulting book: Ven. Lhakdor, Ven. Kelsang Damdul, Lama Lobsang Ngodup, Dawa Tsering, Rinchen Dharlo, Thubten Jinpa, Ming-yee Wang, Jamyang Rinchen, Beata Tikos, Jeffrey Kung, Virginia Tan, Lindley Hanlon, Steven Lane, Tim Moffatt, Diana Stark, Diana Liao, Sandra Li, Luisa Chen, and finally Mr. Kao Chuan De, who graciously provided all the stage props and *thankas* during the three-day event.

May the merits derived from this book bring harmony and peace in the world and joy to welcome the new millennium.

Venerable Guo-gu Bhikshu
New York, 1999

# *NOTES TO THE READER*

With the exception of proper names, all foreign words not included in the *Webster's Unabridged Dictionary* are italicized the first time they appear in this book. Titles of scriptures are all italicized.

Sanskrit words are spelled in English as they are pronounced. The *pinyin* romanization system is adopted for all Chinese terms. The common spellings of Tibetan transliterations of Buddhist terms are adopted throughout the book. However, a few exceptions were permitted where a modified version of the Turrel Wylie system was adopted; no diacritical marks were used.

All important technical terms, titles of scriptures, and foreign words, whether italicized or not, can be found in the glossary.

# A Brief Introduction to Tibetan Buddhism

*His Holiness the 14th Dalai Lama*

I offer the following concise teachings as a foundation for an understanding of the structure and practice of Tibetan Buddhism. I have nothing to say that has not been said before. Do not look upon these teachings as mere information, but as essential teachings on a path leading to the transformation of your mind. Only then will these teachings be of true benefit.

Before Buddhism arrived, the Bon religion was widespread in Tibet. Until recently, Bon study centers still existed in Tibet. Not an effective religion at first, Bon was greatly enriched by Buddhist belief and practice. Around the eighth century CE, King Lha-Tho-Ri Nyen-Tsen introduced Buddhism to Tibet. Since then, Buddhism has spread steadily. Over the course of time, many Indian *pandits* (scholars) came to Tibet and translated sutras, Tantric texts, and commentaries.

During the reign of the irreligious King Lang-Dar-Mar in the 10th century CE, Buddhism suffered a setback, but that eclipse was short-lived. Buddhism soon revived and spread again, starting in the western and eastern parts of Tibet; Indian and Tibetan scholars were again busy translating religious texts. As the number of Tibetan Buddhist scholars grew, the number of visiting Indian scholars gradually declined.

Thus, in the later period of Tibetan Buddhism, our religion developed independently of the later school of Indian Buddhism, although it retained the foundations of the Buddha's teachings. In its essentials, Tibetan Buddhism never suffered alterations or additions at the hands of Tibetan lamas. Their commentaries are clearly identifiable as commentaries, and for their authority, they referred to the main teachings of Lord Buddha or the works of the Indian pandits. For this reason, I do not think it is correct to regard Tibetan Buddhism as separate from the original Indian Buddhism, or to refer to it as lamaism.

## *The Four Noble Truths*

Buddha said, "This is true suffering; this is the true cause; this is true cessation; this is the true path." He also said, "Know the nature of suffering; give up the causes of suffering; attain the cessation of suffering; follow the true path." And he said, "Know suffering, although there is nothing to know. Relinquish the causes of misery, although there is nothing to relinquish. Be earnest in pursuit of cessation, although there is nothing to cease. Practice the means of cessation, although there is nothing to practice." These are three views of the intrinsic nature, action, and ultimate result of the Four Noble Truths.

In the third century CE, the Indian Nagarjuna expounded the philosophy of the Middle Way, which has become central to all schools of Mahayana Buddhism. The Middle Way teaches that "true suffering" derives from samsara, the cycle of birth and rebirth that arises from karma, the retribution for actions stemming from ignorance and delusion. "True cause" means karma and delusion, which are the true causes of suffering. "True cessation" means the complete disappearance of the two preceding conditions. The "true path" is the one path by which we arrive at true cessation.

## *Hinayana*

To attain nirvana, we must follow a prescribed path: the true path, or the Four Noble Truths. Hinayana and Mahayana represent two schools of thought by which we discern this path. According to Hinayana, the so-called Smaller Vehicle, whose practitioners seek nirvana for their own sake, the mind should be trained to exercise a will strong enough to renounce samsara. The practitioner should pursue religious ethics and simultaneously practice meditative absorption and insight so that delusion and its seeds may be purged, ultimately, never to grow again. Thus, we attain nirvana. The paths to be followed are the Paths of Preparation, Application, Seeing, Practice, and Fulfillment.

## *Mahayana*

Followers of Mahayana, the so-called Greater Vehicle, aim at attaining the highest stage of nirvana—buddhahood. They do this not only for themselves but also for all sentient beings. Motivated by the aspiration of Enlightenment and by compassion for all sentient beings, Mahayanists follow almost the same path as Hinayanists, but they also practice other expedient means such as the Six Perfections. By these methods, they seek to rid themselves of delusion as well as the defilement of karmic imprints, thereby working to attain buddhahood. Although the five paths are the same for both vehicles—Preparation, Application, Seeing, Practice, and Fulfillment—a qualitative difference is that Mahayana emphasizes the motivation to benefit all beings. It is said that Hinayanists who have achieved nirvana will eventually adopt methods to attain buddhahood.

## *Tantrayana*

The paths I have mentioned are doctrinal paths that aspirants must follow to provide a sound foundation before practicing *Tantrayana*, the way of yogic methods. The Tibetan School took great care before introducing any tantric doctrine. Spiritual teachers always investigated whether the doctrine was among those the Buddha preached. Competent pandits submitted it to logical analysis, and tested it in the light of experience, before confirming its authenticity and adopting it. This process was necessary because there were many non-Buddhist tantric doctrines that were apt to be confused with those of Buddhism because of their superficial resemblance.

Tantrayana falls into four classes and includes a vast number of treatises that cannot be enumerated here. In the simplest terms, according to this system as already explained, negative karma is considered the cause of the various kinds of misery we suffer. Negative karma results from delusion, which is essentially the product of an undisciplined mind. Therefore, the mind needs to be disciplined and controlled by exercises that stop the flow of harmful and negative thoughts. This flow can be stopped and the wandering or projecting mind brought to rest by concentration on the makeup of one's mind.

One can also focus one's mind on external objects to diminish negative thoughts. For this practice, one needs strong contemplative powers. The figures of deities have been found to be the most suitable objects, thus resulting in many images of deities in Tantrayana. In some cases, progress is achieved through strong faith and devotion; but generally, progress is achieved through the power of reason. And, if one follows the transcendental path of Tantrayana, reason itself will inspire heartfelt conviction.

## *An Outline of the Practice Method of Buddhism*

The perfection of Buddhist practice is achieved not merely through superficial changes, such as leading a monastic life or reciting sacred texts. Whether these activities in themselves should even be called religious is open to question, for religion should be practiced in the mind. If one has the right mental attitude, all activities, bodily action, and speech can be religious. But if one lacks the right attitude—that is, if one does not know how to think properly—one will achieve nothing, even if one's whole life is spent in monasteries reading the scriptures. The first requirement of Buddhist practice, therefore, is transformation of mental attitude. One should take the Three Jewels—Buddha, Dharma, and Sangha—as the final refuge, take into account the laws of karma and its consequences, and cultivate thoughts that will benefit others.

Being earnest in renouncing worldly interests, a practitioner will find great joy. Many followers of the Tibetan school have renounced the world in this way, and they possess an indescribable mental and physical satisfaction. However, such renunciation of the world is not possible for everybody, because it requires great sacrifice. What kind of Dharma can we prescribe for ordinary people? Ruling out immoral acts, any activity that is useful and productive in promoting the happiness of others can certainly go together with practicing the Dharma. Salvation can be achieved by merely leading a household life. We have a saying: "People who make no mental effort, even if they remain in mountain retreats, are only accumulating causes for a descent into hell."

There is an old Tibetan story. Long ago, there was a famous lama named Drom. One day, Drom saw a man walking around a stupa. "It is good for you to walk around the stupa," Drom said, "but wouldn't it be better if you practiced religion?" The man said to himself, "I had better read a holy book then." And so he started a laborious course of reading. One day, Drom happened to see him again. "Reading from a holy book is, of course, good," Drom said, "but wouldn't it be better if you practiced religion?"

The man thought: "It seems even recitation is not good enough. How about meditating?" Not long after, Drom saw him in meditation. He said, "I admit that meditation is good. But wouldn't it really be better if you practiced religion?"

The man was bewildered. "What do you mean by practicing religion? Tell me how it is done."

"Turn your mind away from the forms of this worldly life," Drom told him, "and turn your life towards religion."

Perhaps I may conclude with a brief outline of the Buddhist path in terms of the Three Higher Trainings: Training in Higher Conduct, Training in Higher Meditation, and Training in Higher Wisdom.

### *Training in Higher Conduct*

Training in Higher Conduct, which is the foundation of all the precepts, has many aspects. All are based on the avoidance of the ten non-virtues—three of the body, four of speech, and three of the mind.

The three non-virtues pertaining to the body are:

1. Taking the life of any living being, from humans to the smallest insect, whether directly or indirectly
2. Stealing or taking without consent another's property, directly or indirectly, whatever its value
3. Committing adultery and indulging in perverted forms of sexual intercourse

The four non-virtues pertaining to speech are:

1. Being guilty of falsehood by giving others false or wrong advice, information, or physical indications
2. Being guilty of calumny by causing disunity where unity exists and by aggravating disunity where it already exists
3. Using harsh and abusive language
4. Indulging in gossip out of sheer lust and passion

The three non-virtues pertaining to functions of the mind are:

1. Coveting, or desiring to possess, something that belongs to others
2. Wanting to harm others
3. Doubting the teaching on rebirth, the reality of karma, and the Three Refuges

*Training in Higher Meditation*

Training in Higher Meditation helps the practitioner fix the mind on a single object and develop "mental quiescence" or *shamata*. The technique consists of withdrawing the mind gradually from sense objects and conceptual notions so that the mind becomes unwavering, steady, and calm. Such a mind can concentrate on any object of merit with ease.

To accomplish such a state of realization, many prerequisites are necessary. To be brief, according to Bodhisattva Maitreya, practitioners must avoid the Five Shortcomings and cultivate the Eight Introspective Mental Attitudes.

The Five Shortcomings are:

1. Laxity resulting from a lethargic attitude toward meditation
2. Forgetfulness of the meditation object
3. Distractions of the mind—usually lust
4. Inability to prevent these distractions
5. Imaginary interruptions and the use of false countermeasures

The Eight Introspective Mental Attitudes are:

1. Conviction in the virtue of meditation and the ability to discern shortcomings
2. The earnest desire to meditate and the ability to do so
3. Perseverance and a joyful frame of mind

4. Experience of mental and physical pliancy
5. Conscientious effort to focus on the object of meditation
6. Awareness of any inclination toward sluggishness or intense agitation
7. Immediate readiness to counter distraction the moment it is perceived
8. Relaxation of countermeasures when the objective is already accomplished

The Nine Stages of Concentration are:

1. Fixing the mind on the object of concentration
2. Endeavoring to prolong the concentration
3. Perceiving immediately any diversion of the mind and bringing it back to the object of concentration
4. Maintaining a clear conception of even the minutest detail of the object
5. Strengthening the effort by realizing its virtues
6. Dispelling any adverse feeling towards meditation
7. Maintaining equanimity by dispelling disturbances
8. Taking concentration to its furthest limit
9. Abiding in meditative equipoise without assistance or the effort of memory or consciousness

*Training in Higher Wisdom*

Training in higher wisdom is concerned with developing two kinds of wisdom:

1. Wisdom that comprehends the relative nature of things, or empirical knowledge
2. Wisdom that comprehends the absolute nature of things, or transcendental knowledge

I will briefly describe one more type of wisdom here: the wisdom that destroys all moral and mental defilements, and destroys defilements caused by the power of discriminative thought—the wisdom that comprehends shunyata.

*Shunyata*

Shunyata, the nature of emptiness, is the ultimate reality of all objects, material and phenomenal. Shunyata is neither affected by the powers of the Buddhas, nor dependent on the karmic fruits of sentient beings. Shunyata simply exists, and its nature pervades all elements. Accordingly, by their very nature, all dharmas are empty. To quote from a sutra, "Whether the Buddhas appear in this world or not, shunyata, the ultimate nature of all objects, is absolute and eternal." Shunyata is the negation of a permanent self and of independent existence.

# A Dialogue on Tibetan and Chinese Buddhism

*H. H. the 14th Dalai Lama*
*Venerable Chan Master Sheng-yen*

*Venerable Sheng-yen*:

Buddhism was transmitted from India to China in the second century of the Common Era and to Tibet in the seventh or eighth century CE. Because of distinctive cultural influences and modes of thought, such as Confucianism and Taoism in China and the Bon religion in Tibet, Chinese and Tibetan Buddhism gradually blossomed into very distinctive forms of Buddhism.

Without free exchange of views and frequent interaction, the two traditions in the past, misunderstood and criticized each other. For example, some Chinese Buddhists have thought that Tibetan Buddhism emphasizes esotericism and is therefore obscure and inaccessible, and some Tibetan Buddhists may have regarded Chinese Buddhism as incomplete.

These two Buddhist traditions are really like the separated children of one mother. Because they have been apart for a long time and are now reunited, it is important that they encourage, and work towards, mutual understanding. After hearing the teachings of His Holiness during the past two days, I feel that Tibetan Buddhism is rich in its explication of Dharma, especially the stages of practice, and in its detailed elaboration of doctrinal classification and methods of practice.

*His Holiness*:

I am very happy to have this opportunity to participate in a discussion with Venerable Master Sheng-yen. I first met him in Taiwan in 1997 and have since then met him on a number of occasions. This is the first time that I have had a dialogue with a Chan Buddhist. It is very important for all the different major religious traditions of the world to have this kind of dialogue, so that there can be mutual learning and mutual appreciation of the key tenets and teachings of each other's traditions. This is particularly important for members of all the various Buddhist lineages. Of course, all Buddhists follow the same master, our original teacher Shakyamuni Buddha.

## *The Chan Tradition*

*Venerable Sheng-yen*:

To begin the process of finding common ground between these two great Buddhist traditions, I will briefly outline the development of Chan Buddhism. After its arrival from India in the second century CE, Chinese Buddhism evolved into ten schools, eight of which belong to the Mahayana tradition and two to the Hinayana. Among the Indian Mahayana schools, there were three direct descendants in China: the Three-Treatise School, the Consciousness-Only School, and the Vinaya School.

## *The Union of the Tiantai and Huayan Schools*

*Venerable Sheng-yen*:

In the early formations of Chinese Buddhism, two main schools contributed to the sinification of Indian Buddhism: the Tiantai School and the Huayan School. Both of these schools have very systematic and comprehensive doctrinal classifications. Their presentations of methods of practice are detailed and extremely rich.

Both of these schools relied heavily on Indian sutras and *shastras*. I will not elaborate on these two traditions, except to say that the founder of the Tiantai School, Master Zhiyi, was famous for his development of Nagarjuna's teaching on the two ways reality can be perceived according to the Threefold Truths. The Threefold Truths are the teachings on emptiness, conventional existence, and the Middle Way. On this basis, he also systematized a variety of shamata and *vipashyana* practices. Many of these practices are similar to the Tibetan *Lam Rim* teaching. The Tiantai School based its main tenets on the *Lotus Sutra* and the *Treatise of the Middle Way*, by Nagarjuna Bodhisattva.

The Huayan School teaches the equality, mutual identity, and inclusiveness of all things. It is perhaps best known for its philosophy of the Fourfold Dimensions of Reality:

1. The teaching that reveals the realm of phenomena based on the doctrine of Hinayana
2. The teaching on the underlying principle of phenomena based on the doctrine of the Consciousness-Only and the Middle Way schools
3. The teaching on the unobstructed interrelation between principle and phenomena based on scriptures such as the *Vimalakirti Sutra*
4. The teachings of the unobstructed interrelation between each

> and every phenomenon based on the *Avatamsaka Sutra*, from which the Huayan School took its name

Thus, the Huayan teaching is really a harmonization of all systems of thought within Indian Buddhism. In addition to the *Avatamsaka Sutra* or the *Flower Ornament Scripture*, the Huayan School also appropriated teachings from the *Commentary on the Sutra of the Great Transcendent Wisdom*, by Nagarjuna, and the *Ten Stages of the Bodhisattva Scripture.*

Chan [later transmitted to Japan as Zen] is a kind of culmination of these two schools, synthesizing the best of both traditions in its main teaching. Furthermore, since the emergence of the Chan School, it has gone through several periods of transformation. Without going into the details of such transformation, we can simply summarize that the development and maturation of the thought and practice of Chan made it the dominant school of Chinese Buddhism. However, all three schools—Tiantai, Huayan, and Chan—are based on the teachings of the early scriptures such as the *Agamas* and the *Treasure of Manifest Knowledge.*

## *The Harmonizing and Unifying of Chinese Buddhism*

*Venerable Sheng-yen*:

The characteristic Chinese thought pattern favors inclusiveness, directness, simplicity, and avoidance of meticulous, complex thoughts. Probably the most influential and illustrious figure in the history of the Chan School was the Sixth Patriarch, Huineng. The wisdom of

Huineng—in particular, that gathered in the *Platform Sutra*—reflects this characteristic pattern of thought, which harmonizes and unifies all of the main tenets of Chinese Buddhism. The story of Huineng's own enlightenment is interesting in this regard. One day, he overheard the words from the *Diamond Sutra* "Not abiding anywhere, give rise to mind!" This single line revealed to him the heart of Mahayana Buddhism—emptiness and compassion.

Two other sutras that contributed to the development of Chan are the *Lankavatara Sutra* and the *Vimalakirti Sutra*. The main teaching of the *Lankavatara Sutra* is the idea of *Tathagatagarbha*, or buddha-nature—that we are all endowed with the potential to reach buddhahood. The *Vimalakirti Sutra* reveals that in order to reach genuine enlightenment, practitioners must relinquish attachment and dualistic discrimination. In other words, we must put down all of our afflictive emotions, or kleshas.

To shatter the shackle of kleshas is to be free of all obstructions to the Buddha's insight into the nature of reality. Only then will one know, for the first time, the non-duality of afflictions and wisdom, samsara and nirvana, good and bad. Being free from contrivance and abstract conceptualization, one can be in perfect accordance with what the Buddha sees and what the Buddha knows.

The methods of the Chan School vary from teacher to teacher. In early Chan stories, Bodhidharma, the first Buddhist Patriarch in China, had an interesting dialogue with his student Huike, who became the second Patriarch. One day, Huike sought out the help of Bodhidharma to pacify his afflicted and vexed mind. Bodhidharma told him, "Bring me your mind and I will pacify it!" When Huike could not demonstrate his mind, Bodhidharma said, "There, I have already pacified your mind." Upon hearing this, Huike was greatly enlightened.

In essence, we see a similar dynamic functioning of wisdom in Bodhisattva Manjushri. In one sutra, someone asks Manjushri, "You are the teacher of Buddhas in the past, present, and future. When will you yourself attain buddhahood? And how long have you been cultivating the Dharma?" Bodhisattva Manjushri's reply was quite interesting and unusual: "How long do *you* plan to ask such questions?"

The enlightenment of which Chan masters speak is not attained by any fixed method. The main point is to understand and recognize the mind of kleshas, or mental afflictions. The traditional methods of practice in Indian Buddhism were indeed quite difficult; one had to proceed by practicing the five methods of stilling the mind, beginning with counting one's breath. Then, one progressed through the stages of investigation, waiting, joy, and bliss before reaching meditative equipoise or mental quiescence. In this view, buddhahood was a distant goal indeed!

The teaching of Chan aims at freeing oneself from dualistic deluded thinking. When discriminations arise, when we persist in labeling something as good or bad, as a like or a dislike, we then must try to locate this mind. In the immediacy of the present moment and dropping all clinging, when one cannot find this discriminating mind, it is possible to gain a realization of emptiness.

Hearing this, some people may conclude that Chan practice is a "shortcut" for the lazy. By no means! Chan also requires cultivation of precepts, concentration, and wisdom. If one's mind is not pure, one's conduct will not be pure. Therefore, one must begin by cultivating the precepts individually. Cultivating precepts simply means doing what one should do and not doing what one should not do. At the same time, if one truly wants to practice Chan, *bodhichitta*—arousing the mind of altruism to benefit others—is necessary. To do this, one should receive the bodhisattva precepts and take to heart the Three Cumulative Pure Precepts of a bodhisattva.

The Three Cumulative Pure Precepts are ending all non-virtue, cultivating all goodness, and delivering all sentient beings. In fact, I believe that these Three Cumulative Pure Precepts are in perfect harmony with the teaching of the Three Principle Paths: renunciation, bodhi-mind, and the correct view of emptiness, as taught by His Holiness.

If a person has already seen buddha-nature—the nature of emptiness—and has eradicated all afflictions of mind, formalities and sectarian rules of conduct become useless because all conduct naturally will accord with the precepts. For example, the great Chan Master Baizhang (720-814) said that he had not violated the precepts of the Buddhist path, nor would he allow himself to be bound by them. We should note that Master Baizhang was famous for establishing an early set of rules for Chan monastic discipline, called the *Pure Rules of Baizhang,* which in essence replaced the Indian codes of conduct for monks,

Regarding the realizations of samadhi and prajna, perhaps I should point out that when Chan speaks of great samadhi, it is in essence inseparable from prajna, or wisdom. Chan does not place much emphasis on the progressive stages of mental quiescence leading to samadhi. Instead, Chan places greater emphasis on the simultaneous realization of samadhi and wisdom—if the realization of emptiness dawns, great samadhi also manifests. Samadhi and prajna are mutually inclusive and equal.

How one actually engages in the practice of Chan depends on one's conviction and faith. One should have resolute faith in the words of the Buddha that we all have buddha-nature—that we all have the full potential to be Buddhas. If in an instant of thought we can be free from dualistic discriminations, it is possible to be enlightened right then! We see in the early scriptures such as the *Agamas* that in the Buddha's time many people reached arhatship upon hearing a simple phrase from the Buddha. For example, in the case of one layperson who went to see Shakyamuni Buddha, all that the Buddha said was "Good, good. It is good that you have come now," and that person immediately reached arhatship! In Chan, there were many such cases, including the case of Master Huineng, who experienced sudden enlightenment when he heard the *Diamond Sutra*.

However, ordinary people who are unable to do this must begin with the basics. In terms of meditation, the first thing people should cultivate is a relaxed body and mind. To accomplish this, it is sufficient to use the method of counting the breath or some other method. On this basis, people can proceed to use either one of the two advanced Chan meditation methods, those of the Caodong and Linji schools. The Caodong School of Chan teaches the method of silent illumination. One begins by maintaining a simple awareness of one's own bodily sensations and presence in the act of "just sitting." Then, one rests on the awareness of mind itself. When the mind is stable, one's awareness continues, reaching a state of "cessation-contemplation." No numbers, no body, no environment, no theme at all occupies the mind. This is a kind of formless contemplation apart from the four elements, the five aggregates, and levels of consciousness. At this time, one can realize who one really is in the nature of reality.

To restate simply: whatever internal or external experiences that may arise should all be left behind, and one should free oneself from all concepts, labels, descriptions, and comparisons. Without giving rise to discriminating thoughts, one should maintain the utmost clarity.

Many people like talking about enlightenment. They think that the extemporaneous acts of ancient Chan masters, such as hitting people or yelling at them, can bring enlightenment, that these events can free them from wandering thoughts and afflictions. However, these rare actions in the Chan School are only useful when a highly accomplished student is vexed, in the midst of discrimination, by strong attachments. Such sudden, drastic measures are useful only when the causes and conditions are ripe. Even then, the student's experience may not necessarily be enlightenment.

If these methods are not appropriate or useful, there is also the *huatou* or the *gongan* method of the Linji School of Chan. One can ask such questions as "Who is having so many afflictions?" "Who is clinging and engaging in wandering thoughts?" "Who has this karma?" "Who is it?" When one continually and single-mindedly asks such questions, it is possible to congeal all of the wandering thoughts, vexations, and ignorance until they do not arise. At that point, realizing the student's state of mind, a skillful master may do or say something out of the ordinary to precipitate the student's experience of emptiness.

## *Building a Pure Land in the World*

*Venerable Sheng-yen*:

This purification of our minds and actions is a prerequisite to our purification of the larger realms of the world as a whole. I am currently involved in a social movement, "Building a Pure Land in the World." It is our hope to make the Buddha Land manifest in the human world. To make this vision come true, we must begin by purifying our minds and then purifying our actions. When our minds and our actions are pure, we will be able to have a profound influence on others, enabling their minds and actions to be pure. Eventually, in this way, our world will become a Pure Land.

Purity refers to a state free from self-grasping vexations. To purify the mind is indeed very difficult. A true realization of pure mind, free from afflictive emotions, actually begins after one has experienced the wisdom of emptiness. Though this is a difficult path, we should not be discouraged and give up hope. Practice always begins with being an ordinary person. We begin our practice because we have afflictive emotions. Indeed, if we do not have these vexations, we would have no idea about starting to practice.

According to the Tiantai School, a single thought-moment in our mind is connected to the minds of all sentient beings everywhere. Even if we cannot immediately be in accordance with the wisdom of emptiness, at least we can avoid acting on our vexations. To be free from afflictions temporarily is much better than churning in the sea of suffering!

The process of curing the disease of vexation has three stages: recognition, subduing, and severance. The ability to recognize our confusion and ignorance is already an improvement. Only after recognizing what vexations are can we begin to subdue them. Then, we can really sever them. If one knows one's vexations, one is already in consonance with the pure mind.

For this reason, as soon as we recognize the mind of kleshas or emotional turmoil, we should immediately put this mind down. We can choose to use the mindfulness-of-breath method, the silent illumination method, or the huatou or gongan method to allow our wandering, vexed minds to settle down. At this moment, our minds are in accordance with pure buddha-nature.

The Buddha teaches that a single pure thought constitutes a moment of buddhahood; at that moment, one is a Buddha. The *Lotus Sutra* expresses this idea clearly when it states that a person can attain buddhahood by entering a temple and reciting "Homage to the Buddha" just once. However, this person can only be called a "causal buddha," not a buddha of the "fruition level." In other words, one who has a single pure thought in consonance with intrinsic buddha-nature is manifesting the causal ground of buddhahood, which we all possess. However, this is not the same as realizing buddhahood through the fruition of practice.

When we all develop faith in this truth, goodness will flow from our actions; our world will become a Buddha Land.

## *The Tibetan Tradition*

*His Holiness*:

Earlier today in our private meeting, I was very impressed and pleased to hear that Venerable Sheng-yen once spent six years in solitary retreat. Listening to your presentation of Chan Buddhist teachings, my immediate and very profound feeling was that I was listening to words of wisdom from someone who is very experienced and a great practitioner. For all of us, to have knowledge of Dharma is indeed very important, but perhaps what is more important is to put that knowledge of Dharma into practice.

Listening to your explanation of Chan Buddhism, I jotted down a few questions that I would like to ask. First, in which century did Master Huineng live?

*Venerable Sheng-yen*:

He lived in the eighth century of the Common Era.

*His Holiness*:

The reason I ask is that there is some historical connection to Chan in the origin and development of Tibetan Buddhism. We know that Lama Tsongkhapa had been one of the most vocal critics of the sudden teachings of Chan in Tibet, and there was a great debate surrounding Chan and the teachings transmitted from Indian Buddhism.

However, in the Samye Temple during the formative era of Tibetan Buddhism in the reign of King Tri-song-Deutsen, different wings were devoted to different practices. One section is devoted to the *Vajrayana* practitioners—the *tantricas*. Another section is dedicated to the *lozawas* and the panditas—the translators and the scholars. The third section is called the dhyana hall, the place of meditation. This is supposed to have been the residence of a Chinese master referred to as Hoshang. It was during the eighth century, when Samye was built, that the Indian masters Santarakshita and Kamalashila were active in Tibet and were part of the development of Tibetan Buddhism.

My feeling is that if Santarakshita built a separate wing in the Samye temple for the residence of the Chinese Chan masters, he must have welcomed that tradition and recognized it as an important element of Buddhism in Tibet. However, it seems that during the time of his disciple, Kamalashila, certain followers of Chan in Tibet perhaps promoted a slightly different version of the original doctrine. They placed tremendous emphasis on rejecting all forms of thought, not just in the context of a specific practice, but almost as a philosophical position. This is what Kamalashila attacked. Therefore, it seems to me, there were two different versions of Chan that came to Tibet.

*Venerable Sheng-yen*:

I am very grateful to His Holiness for bringing up the subject of the Chinese master Hoshang. From the story, it seems that those Chinese monks during the time of Kamalashila were not qualified to represent Chan. In the Dun Huang Caves, a place where many Buddhist texts were excavated, Buddhist scholars have found ancient texts relating a similar story about the first Chinese monk who greatly influenced Tibetan Buddhism, in particular the practice of meditation. So maybe the first Chinese master who went to Tibet wasn't so bad after all!

*His Holiness*:

In the Tibetan story, the first Chinese master was welcome; the second master supposedly lost the debate!

*Venerable Sheng-yen*:

So maybe the problem will not be with me, but with my successor who will again lose!

*His Holiness*:

Yes! From the Tibetan viewpoint, we welcome the first Hoshang. To the followers of the second Hoshang, we will have to say "good-bye!" If the Chinese masters that we encounter now are followers of the first Chinese master in Tibet, we will gladly receive them. If they are followers of the second Chinese master, we will have to say "farewell."

I do not personally feel that there is a real contradiction between the approaches of the gradual path and the sudden path. However, this is not to say that the sudden path will be appropriate for everyone. There may be exceptional circumstances in which certain individuals may gain greater benefit from an approach that is spontaneous, simultaneous, and instantaneous, but generally speaking, the gradual approach is probably more appropriate.

*Venerable Sheng-yen*:

I agree with what His Holiness has just said about instantaneous enlightenment and gradual practice. I should, however, caution people not to think that only very well educated people of the highest intellectual caliber can practice the instantaneous approach. In fact, sometimes the instantaneous approach can be useful for people who have no education. An example of this was the Sixth Patriarch Huineng. Although he was illiterate, he demonstrated a profound grasp of the Dharma.

A similar story happened at the time of the Buddha. Suddhipanthaka, one of the Buddha's disciples, was a person of very low intelligence who understood none of the teachings. However, he attained arhatship following a method the Buddha taught him: sweeping floors and cleaning shoes!

*His Holiness*:

Here I would like to clarify one point. In Buddhism, we find a lot of emphasis on wisdom, intelligence, and insight. Sometimes the impression is given that we are talking about brainy people, people with a high caliber of brainpower, but this is not necessarily the meaning of wisdom or insight in the Buddhist context. In the Buddhist scriptures, there are descriptions of intelligence gone berserk, where persons have gone to the extreme of analysis yet simply do not have any insight, just a lot of clever ideas. Wisdom need not include intelligence but has more to do with insight and knowledge.

Second, I would like to point out that there might be people whom we would not call clever or brainy, but who may have the necessary focus and power. As for the story of the monk who was very dull, we can see that by sweeping the floor and cleaning shoes, Suddhipanthaka increased his level of wisdom and knowledge.

You spoke about Chan Buddhism and some of the key teachings of the Chan tradition. In Tibetan texts, we do find references to the Chan method, particularly the sudden or instantaneous approach. For example, I can remember a text from the Kagyupa tradition that has a very explicit statement on the practice of *mahamudra* as a sudden path, stating that those who understand mahamudra in a gradualistic way are completely deluded! Indeed, there is such a thing as a sudden approach to realization, which is spontaneous and not limited to the structure of gradual practice.

We also find such expressions as "simultaneity of knowledge and liberation" in the writings of the Sakyapa tradition, particularly in the practice of *rdzogs-chen* [pronounced Zog chen] of the Nyingmapa tradition. In the Gelugpa tradition, even Lama Tsongkhapa accepts the notion of simultaneity and instantaneous liberation. However, he points out that what actually seems like an instantaneous realization is actually a culmination of many factors suddenly coming into play, leading to that moment of liberation.

Lama Tsongkhapa gives an example from a sutra relating the story of a king from central India who received a very expensive gift from the king of a distant kingdom. The king did not know what gift to send in return because he felt that the gift he had received was so valuable. Finally, he approached the Buddha and asked for advice. The Buddha suggested that the king send a painting of the Wheel of Life depicting the twelve links of dependent origination together with a description in verse form. The king sent that gift with the message "You should receive this gift with great joy and festivity."

The other king was quite curious when he got the verbal message, but he made all the arrangements to receive this gift with great festivity. When he finally opened the gift, he was quite surprised to see that it was such a small painting. He looked at the painting and began to understand the image, and when he read the descriptions of the twelve links of dependent origination depicted in the Wheel of Life, he instantaneously realized its truth. This experience occurred suddenly, out of the blue, simply as a result of the visual experience of the painting and a statement of its meaning. From Lama Tsongkhapa's point of view, although the actual event may be instantaneous, it is the result of many factors coming together. The final, momentary event operates as a spark, a catalyst.

In the Tibetan tradition, masters do not use the stick, as the Chinese master did in your story, but in the rdzogs-chen teaching, there is a similar approach, wherein the practitioner shouts the syllable "peh!" with great force. It is said that when the syllable is uttered, the whole chain of thought processes is instantly cut off, and the practitioner experiences a sudden, spontaneous realization. This experience is described as a sense of wonderment and non-conceptuality—a state free of thoughts.

*Venerable Sheng-yen*:

Will the practitioner remain in this state of wonderment? Is it just a momentary experience, or is it a prolonged experience?

*His Holiness*:

In response to this, there is a verse attributed to Sakya Pandita, saying that between the gaps of different thought processes, inner radiance or clear-light takes place continuously. The verse suggests that when you shout "peh" and experience this sudden spontaneous sense of wonderment and non-conceptuality, what you experience is this clear-light, which you also call emptiness. However, this experience is only momentary. It is also said that those who have great accumulations of merit can experience emptiness when all the conditions are ripened. In the rdzogs-chen teaching, if your wonderment is accompanied by blessings and inspirations from your guru, and possessing a much higher store of merits, you will be able to perfect that experience into *rigpa*, true pristine awareness. When you experience this clear light, the whole world fuses into the nature of emptiness, or ultimate reality.

*Venerable Sheng-yen*:

How long can the individual maintain this state of clear-light and perceive the nature of emptiness? Does this experience gradually fade away? Can the person experience other afflictions of the mind? How does this experience affect one's dream state?

*His Holiness*:

Again using the rdzogs-chen terminology, when we talk about the clear-light nature of mind, we are actually talking about an essential quality of consciousness, which is continually without interruption. By analogy, so long as there is water, the clear nature of water will remain. Of course, sometimes the water is muddied and we cannot see its essential clarity. So, when we stir the water, it becomes more muddied. In order to perceive the clear nature of the water, you have to let it lie still. Once you stop stirring the water and let it lie still, it will regain its clear nature. So it is only by stilling that muddied water that you will see the clarity of the water. The clarity of the water does not exist somewhere outside the muddied water.

Similarly, whether one has a virtuous thought or a non-virtuous thought, one is still in the state of mind pervaded by the clear-light nature. From the viewpoint of practice, both virtuous and non-virtuous thoughts are obstructions to experiencing clear-light. Therefore, we place the emphasis on trying to still one's consciousness, on stopping both the virtuous and the non-virtuous thought processes. Only then will one experience the clear-light. We can see a lot of similarities or parallels between these teachings and those of the sudden, simultaneous approach of Chan Buddhism.

Once an individual is able to have conscious experiences of clear-light, there will be an immediate effect on the clarity of one's dreams. However, such rdzogs-chen approaches to instantaneous teachings require preliminary practices called "Seeking the true face of mind." One does this by analyzing the mind's origin, abidance, and dissolution or disappearance. Here, the analysis is quite similar to the four-cornered logic of the Madhyamika *tetralemma*, or fourfold analysis.

In the Tibetan tradition, there are also discussions of the simultaneous attainment of shamata and vipashyana. But to attain this level, the practitioner would have to reach at least the eighth level of mental development as the result of tantric meditation and Vajrayana practices. Only then can the practitioner attain shamata and vipashyana simultaneously.

You described a form of Chan meditation where the practitioner is encouraged to search for that "I" who experiences the negative afflictions through questions such as "Who am I?" "Who creates this experience?" and so on. That approach is quite similar to the Madhyamika's approach of diamond-splinter analysis, which views things from the perspective of causes and effects. We also find similar approaches in the scriptures on the *seven-point analysis* of personhood or selfhood that Chandrakirti (600-650) used. In the Kagyupa tradition, the great yogi Milarepa (1040-1123) used similar approaches by constantly asking his students to look for themselves: "Where are you?"

I would also like to point out that one of the central teachings of the Middle Way School is to constantly question whether or not things exist in the way they seem to exist. Here, it seems important to understand what emptiness really means. For example, we can say whether, in front of our eyes, an insect exists or not. After close inspection, we may arrive at the opposite conclusion, that there is no insect there. But this absence is not emptiness. So, sometimes finding and not finding seem to coincide. Emptiness is something that is found as a result of subjecting something that exists to close scrutiny and trying to find out what its ultimate nature really is.

*Venerable Sheng-yen*:

Some people think that when they ask themselves "Who am I?" and find an absence of mind, or when they rest in a blank state of mind, that they have reached enlightenment. This is a grave mistake! This state is sometimes in Chan called "stubborn emptiness." A qualified Chan master must confirm the student's experience. In addition, the student must reflect on and observe his or her daily life to see whether there are still many afflictions or strong attachments.

If a person has a genuine glimpse of emptiness, this is called "shallow enlightenment," or "seeing one's self-nature." If the individual can maintain that experience continually without end, we call that thorough enlightenment. However, if the individual's experience does not accord with the nature of emptiness in the Middle Way teaching, we also do not recognize that as true enlightenment.

The realization of no-self is really the result of the practice of non-seeking, because as a person's practice advances, he or she ceases searching for individual enlightenment and concentrates on helping others. When you have ceased to be concerned with your own attainments and are thoroughly involved in efforts to help liberate others from suffering, then there is a possibility of enlightenment.

*His Holiness*:

In Tibetan and Indian Buddhism, there are eight preparatory stages of cultivation of the four meditative absorptions. The purpose of the fifth stage, analysis, is to check whether one has gained control of certain strong emotions. In the case of a man, one would conjure an image of a woman. If at that point a person still has lust, then that person would have to retrain. The point is that one who has attained the first state of absorption has already overcome various attachments and lust. On the other hand, some people have realized emptiness but have not calmed their inclinations to lust, desire, and other attachments, which have so many levels.

Master Sheng-yen, you mentioned that an individual can remain in the experience of emptiness uninterruptedly. Such experience of realization can take place only at a much higher stage of development, because this involves a self-mastery over both meditative equipoise and subsequent realizations. In many of the stages, before one becomes fully enlightened, meditative equipoise and the subsequent realizations are sequential and they alternate. It is said that at the state of full enlightenment, meditative equipoise and the subsequent realizations would become simultaneous. From that point of view, anyone who is able to maintain the direct experience of emptiness in meditative equipoise without ever veering from it is fully enlightened.

*Venerable Sheng-yen*:

Thorough enlightenment is not the same as arhatship. A state of thorough enlightenment does not end afflictions. Rather, it is a state in which doubt with regard to the Dharma is forever terminated. Fully enlightened people may still have afflictions, but they will not manifest them verbally or bodily. They are not free from all afflictions, but they clearly know the path of practice they must follow.

Chan does not emphasize the sequential practice of dhyana. I have personally practiced sequential meditative equipoise or dhyana; however, the personal experience of "seeing self-nature" or emptiness is more important. Like the first taste of water, it is something that you must experience for yourself. The experience of the nature of emptiness is the same. You must experience it personally or you will never know it. You may hear of it, but that is not good enough. Thorough enlightenment, however, differs from seeing self-nature, the initial experience of emptiness, in that you may return to the ordinary state of mind after you see your self-nature and not fully recognize how afflictions operate and manifest. A thoroughly enlightened person, whose mind is extremely clear, is fully aware of the workings of afflictions at all times.

Furthermore, from the Chan point of view, a thoroughly enlightened state is not something that is maintained in meditative equipoise.

Because this is the first time we have had such a dialogue, and we have so very little opportunity, it may not be very easy for us to delve into the details very clearly. It may take two or three days at least to clarify some of these issues.

*His Holiness*:

As the scriptures state, for practitioners who have directly experienced emptiness, its truth is inexpressible, beyond language and words. Without this direct experience, emptiness is only intellectual and conceptual understanding.

I would like to refer to the Master Sheng-yen's new initiative, which involves building the purity of society and the environment around the purity of the individual's mind. I find this very encouraging because it is rather similar to and confirms my own approach. Often, I tell people that as far as liberation from samsara and suffering is concerned, in some sense it is the private business of an individual. However, at the level of community, it is more important to try to create what I would call "the nirvana of society." In this society, strong negative emotions such as hatred, anger, jealousy, and such restless states of mind would be less dominant. So here I think there is a real meeting of minds. I would like to express my thanks for your new initiative.

*Venerable Sheng-yen*:

Talking to His Holiness is not like two beings from different worlds talking to each other! Our language may be different, but the basic ideas and concepts are the same. Thank you.

*His Holiness*:

In the future, it would be wonderful to have more of this kind of dialogue and discussion, especially on emptiness, at Five-Peak Mountain in China.

*Venerable Sheng-yen*:

It is said that Manjushri's place sacred on this Earth is Five-Peak Mountain in China. Welcome everybody, and let's pray that we can return to the mountain soon!

*His Holiness*:

If we had the opportunity to engage in such dialogues on emptiness on Five-Peak Mountain, Manjushri's sacred place, and if we still could not be blessed by Manjushri, perhaps we could conclude that Manjushri is empty!

We can take some questions from the audience.

*Venerable Sheng-yen*:

All the difficult questions should be given to His Holiness!

*Questioner*:

Venerable Sheng-yen, does Chan belong to the Vajrayana teachings or do the Vajrayana teachings belong to Chan?

*Venerable Sheng-yen*:

Because I have never studied Tantra, it is better for His Holiness to answer this question. However, if we say that the two, Tantra and Chan, are really the same, and learning either one of the two is like learning both, then I would have to say that there may be a problem with this idea! There are similarities and differences within the two traditions.

*His Holiness*:

Generally, it is stated that the profundity of the Vajrayana teachings really comes from their sophistication in meditation practices. Therefore, when classifying Vajrayana teachings within the category of the three baskets or three discourses, we see them as part of the sutras. That is because we view the Vajrayana teachings as sophisticated developments of dhyana practices.

*Questioner*:

To engage in the practice of Dharma, first you have to listen, then study, and then contemplate. But it seems that in the practice of emptiness, sometimes faith alone can lead to the experience of wisdom. Is that true?

*Venerable Sheng-yen*:

Let me answer this question first. When Chan Buddhists talk about enlightenment, they distinguish between "enlightenment through intellectual understanding" and "actualized enlightenment" or experiential realization. For example, if seeing dependent-origination means seeing the Dharma, and that also means seeing the Buddha, is that enlightenment? Personally, I would consider that a kind of "enlightenment through intellectual understanding." It is not the same as actualized enlightenment or true realization. Genuine enlightenment requires personal experience of the wisdom of emptiness—prajna.

*His Holiness*:

In general, in the Tibetan tradition we tend to use the word enlightenment to refer to the level of superior beings, the noble "aryas."

*Questioner*:

What is the difference between practicing emptiness and gaining insight into emptiness or gaining enlightenment?

*Venerable Sheng-yen*:

What is the difference or relationship between practice and enlightenment? Those with very sharp karmic potential may be able to attain enlightenment very quickly, but they may still lack certain accumulations of merit and virtue. This means that after their enlightenment they need to continue to practice. As for others, before their enlightenment, at the stage of accumulation, they need to amass the necessary factors such as virtue to reach enlightenment.

*Questioner*:

When you become enlightened, if you are fully enlightened, and if you are a buddha, then there is no need to practice. If there is no need to practice, why do we recite the last line of the prayer, the prayer that we may always be able to engage in bodhisattva deeds?

*His Holiness*:

When we talk about the deeds of the bodhisattva, we can discuss it in two aspects. One aspect is engaging in the bodhisattva deeds to perfect one's self, to attain full enlightenment. Once you become fully enlightened, you do not need to engage in the bodhisattva deeds. The second aspect is that, since your vow is to seek the well-being of other sentient beings, even after your full enlightenment, you will engage in the deeds of the bodhisattva.

*Questioner*:

Master Sheng-yen, in the Chinese Buddhist tradition, is there an understanding of a separate approach to enlightenment outside the framework of the Four Noble Truths; and if so, what is that approach?

*Venerable Sheng-yen*:

There is no separate understanding apart from the Four Noble Truths. However, I should clarify that the sudden enlightenment approach does not include any discussion of a sequential or gradual path. So, if you do not want to take the sequential or gradual path, the best thing may be for you to practice Chan! But this approach does not mean it is easy. It does not mean that you are getting something for nothing. Because even if you are enlightened without going through the gradual path, then even after enlightenment, you have to continue to practice!

As we noted before, some people practice on the causal ground and others on the ground of fruition. Even Shakyamuni Buddha, after attaining buddhahood, practiced meditation daily. I asked His Holiness how he practices every day, because His Holiness is a practitioner of great realization, but he told me that every day he still spends over three hours in meditation and prostration. This is the way of many great masters of the Chan tradition.

*Questioner*:

Master Sheng-yen, what is being negated in the context of understanding emptiness? What, exactly, is being emptied? What is True Suchness?

*Venerable Sheng-yen*:

Emptiness means being free from the two extremes of existence and mere nothingness, nor is one attached to the middle! This is the Middle Way, the teaching of Madhyamika. As for True Suchness, it is a teaching from the Consciousness-Only and the Tathagatagarbha schools. It is very simple to understand True Suchness. When you truly understand vexation, vexation is not different from True Suchness. Foolish people who are enmeshed in all kinds of afflictions all the time and do not recognize them, cannot know True Suchness. If you know your own negative afflictions very well, then you are in accordance with True Suchness. When all afflictions, including the very subtle vexations, have been eliminated, that is buddhahood. So, I have to say that vexation is True Suchness! Without afflictions or vexation, True Suchness has no existence. True Suchness is merely a conventional name. This may be very difficult to understand.

*Questioner:*

Venerable Sheng-yen, can one attain buddhahood with just skillful means or wisdom alone?

*Venerable Sheng-yen:*

[Comment to the translator] "Why do you always pick out ones for me? Give some to His Holiness!" (Laughter in the audience)

*Questioner:*

Is there such a thing as clairvoyance and precognition? Can anyone comment on this?

*His Holiness:*

Often, when I asked questions of my senior tutor Ling Rinpoche, he came up with rather strange, sometimes quite strange answers. One day I began to suspect that he might have other sources of knowledge, so once I asked him directly, "Do you sometimes have clairvoyant experiences?" He said, "I don't know, but sometimes certain types of knowledge seem to arise in me that are rather weird." So, clairvoyance or precognition seems to be a real possibility.

Of course, I have met people who claim to have clairvoyance, but I am rather doubtful and quite skeptical, but Ling Rinpoche is someone I have known since childhood, so I can trust him. But I have also met people who claim to have clairvoyance and precognition and act as if they possess such knowledge, but I must say I am rather skeptical in these cases. When I visited Taiwan, I noticed there was quite a sizable community of Tibetan lamas and monks. I warned them not to pretend to have high realization that they do not possess. Particularly, they should not pretend to have clairvoyant powers or precognition, because their pretense might be revealed.

When talking about precognition or clairvoyance, we can say that theoretically, the ability to know is an inherent property of consciousness and mind, and even in our ordinary experiences, we sometimes have certain premonitions of what might happen. We may have premonitions in the morning, sort of a certain sense of intuition. These, I think, are indications of the seed for such cognitive powers that lie within us. It seems that through the application of meditative practices, and particularly single-pointedness of mind, we begin to sharpen the focus of our memory and mindfulness. In that way, it seems our recollection or ability to recollect experiences becomes stronger and stronger. Once that power of recollection is sharp, the potential for precognition increases. That is at least the theoretical basis for believing in precognition. So, it seems that precognition or clairvoyance seems to arise in different forms in different people.

During the Seventh Dalai Lama's time, there was a highly realized master named Dag-pu-Lobsang-Denbe-Gyaltsen (1714-1762), who was universally recognized as someone with clairvoyant power. Once a great Gelugpa master, Jang-gya-Rolbay-Dorjay (1717-1786), asked him, "How does this knowledge arise in you?" Dag-pu-Lobsang-Denbe-Gyaltsen replied that whenever he had to seriously think about something, a given subject or matter, he would focus on the first image that appeared in his mind, which was usually a bell. On top of that bell would appear certain images, and patterns that arose would give him certain premonitions. Of course, in the Highest Yoga Tantra teachings, there are specific practices that are supposed to enable people to develop that kind of power. The sutras do speak of clairvoyance, but usually based on visual and audio perceptions only—never through olfactory perceptions. Even in our ordinary experiences, we can cognize objects at a distance through our visual perception and audio perception, not through scent. Therefore, the power of clairvoyance is limited.

*Venerable Sheng-yen*:

There are definitely such supernatural powers as clairvoyance, and for a person with faith in the Dharma to deny the existence of such clairvoyance or supernatural power would be inappropriate. But Shakyamuni Buddha warned his disciples not to use such power carelessly. In fact, the Chinese Chan tradition forbids practitioners and masters to use or even to talk about such powers. Relating this ability to ourselves, we see that foolish people hope to gain such supernatural powers so that they can help themselves. People with wisdom, on the other hand, use their own insights to handle affairs in their lives. To use wisdom to resolve problems, all you have to do is use it once. Dealing with problems through supernatural powers yields only temporary solutions; the problems will not only not be resolved, but they will reemerge. This dialogue is called appropriately the "wisdom teachings," not the supernatural teachings.

*His Holiness*:

I would like to take this opportunity to express my special appreciation to Venerable Chan Master Sheng-yen.

*Venerable Sheng-yen*:

Thank you.

—End of dialogue—

# APPENDIX ONE

His Holiness the 14th Dalai Lama is the spiritual and temporal leader of the six million people of Tibet. A great scholar, a man of peace, and a foremost Buddhist teacher, His Holiness refers to himself as a "simple Buddhist monk" whose "real religion is kindness." His Holiness has received many awards for his distinguished world leadership in service of freedom, peace, and nonviolence, as well as widespread recognition for his writings on Buddhist philosophy and science.

In 1989 he was awarded the Nobel Peace Prize for his consistent opposition to the use of violence in the struggle for the liberation of Tibet and its people. His Holiness travels around the world, not only to raise international awareness of the suffering of the Tibetan people, but also to talk about Tibetan Buddhism and the power of compassion.

# APPENDIX TWO

Venerable Chan Master Sheng-yen is one of the foremost scholars and teachers of Chinese Buddhism who has contributed greatly to the revival of Chinese Buddhism.

He was born near Shanghai in 1930 and ordained as a monk in 1943. During the Communist takeover of China in 1949, Venerable Sheng-yen escaped with the Nationalist army to Taiwan. After 15 years of strenuous scriptural study and struggle in his meditation work, at the age of 28, while sojourning at various monasteries in southern Taiwan, he had the deepest spiritual experience of his life. His experience was later recognized by masters in the two main lineages of Chan [Zen], and he became the lineage holder of these two schools of Chinese Buddhism, the Linji and the Caodong.

After spending six years solitary meditation to deepen his practice, Venerable Sheng-yen went to Japan and received his Master's and Doctorate degrees in Buddhist Literature from Rissho University. Since then, he has published over ninety books, available in Chinese, English, and several other languages. Venerable Sheng-yen now divides his time between his centers in New York and monasteries in Taiwan, leading intensive Chan meditation retreats, lecturing, and hosting international Buddhist conferences.

# GLOSSARY

*Agama* (Skt.): The earliest collection of Buddha Shakyamuni's fundamental teachings.

Baizhang Huaihai (720-814): A Chinese Chan master of the Tang Dynasty, a disciple of Mazu Daoyi and teacher of Huangbo Xiyun. Noted for establishing an early set of rules for Chan monastic discipline, called the *Pure Rules of Baizhang*.

*bodhichitta* (Skt.): Literally, "awakened mind." The mind of one who aspires to enlightenment but who at the same time is guided by the intention to help sentient beings.

bodhi-mind: Synonymous with bodhichitta.

bodhisattva (Skt.): Literally, "awakened being," a follower of the Mahayana path who vows to help sentient beings over attaining personal enlightenment.

buddha-nature: The nature or potentiality for buddhahood; synonym for nature of emptiness, tathagatagarbha, and True Suchness. See *tathagatagarbha*.

Caodong (Jap. Soto): Pronounced "tsao dong." One of the two major surviving schools of Chan Buddhism, the other being the Linji (Jap. Rinzai).

Consciousness-Only School (Chn. Weishi): Also known as the Indian Yogachara School, this school holds that all things exist only as presentations or phenomenal appearances that are manifestations of our consciousness.

delusion (Skt. *Avidya*): Also known as fundamental ignorance. It is a mental state that arises from the mistaken perception of reality due to an attachment to a sense of self.

dharma (Skt.): Dharma has two basic meanings. Dharma with an upper case "D" means the Buddhist teaching. Dharma with the lower case "d" simply refers to a thing, an object, and physical or mental phenomenon.

dhyana (Skt.): Meditative concentration, transliterated by the Chinese as *chan'na*. In a specific sense, dhyana refers to the four absorptions, or stages of meditation. In the first, the practitioner dwells in the joy of abandoning coarse desires. In the second, the practitioner dwells solely in the joy of concentration. In the third, the practitioner attains exquisite bliss surpassing that of ordinary concentration. In the fourth, the practitioner dwells in equanimity of mind free from various sensations of pain and pleasure. See samadhi.

*rdzogs-chen* (Tib.): An advanced meditation practice from the Tibetan Nyingma tradition that focuses on the natural empty and luminous quality of mind called *rigpa*.

*Diamond* or the *Vajracchedika Sutra* (Skt.): One of the most popular teachings on the nature of emptiness and the conduct of a bodhisattva.

eight consciousnesses: A central idea from the Indian Yogachara School or the Chinese Consciousness-Only School, which divides consciousness into eight modes of operation. The first five consciousnesses refer to the "knowing" that arises from contacts between the sense faculties and their corresponding sense objects. The sixth consciousness refers to the faculty of discrimination. The seventh consciousness refers to the reality of self-clinging. The eighth consciousness refers to a kind of repository that contains all experiences as karmically charged seeds waiting for conditions to ripen as actions of body, speech, and thought. See karma and Consciousness-Only School.

five methods of stilling the mind: The five methods are contemplating on 1) breath, 2) impurity, 3) loving-kindness, 4) causes and conditions [selflessness], and 5) the boundaries of sense faculties, sense data, and sense consciousness.

Gelugpa (Tib.): One of the four main schools of Tibetan Buddhism, the others being the Sakyapa, Nyingmapa, and Kagyupa.

*gongan* (Chn.): A meditative method in Chan to help students bring their mind to the state of "great doubt" as a precondition for experiencing one's buddha-nature. In Zen, this practice is known as koan.

*Hinayana* (Skt.): Literally, "Lesser Vehicle," the Buddhist path of personal liberation, contrasted to the Mahayana, or the "Great Vehicle", in which the bodhisattva ideal is espoused. The use of this term in Chinese Buddhism is not necessarily pejorative, nor does it refer to any specific practice tradition or region. The term came into being with the development of Mahayana Buddhism and has since been used to distinguish the bodhisattva aspiration to liberate others before liberating oneself.

*Hoshang* (Chn.): Not a person, as sometimes thought by Tibet Buddhists, but a common term for a Chinese Buddhist monastic.

*huatou* (Chn.): Sometimes used interchangeably with *gongan*, a Chan method of meditation. See *gongan.*

Huayan (Chn.): A major school of Chinese Buddhism, active during the end of the Sui and the beginning of the Tang dynasties, based on the *Flower Ornament Scripture,* or the *Avatamsaka Sutra.* The central teaching of this school is that of "totality"—that all things in the universe interpenetrate in mutual identity.

Kagyupa (Tib.): One of the four main schools of Tibetan Buddhism, the others being the Sakyapa, Nyingmapa, and Gelugpa.

karma (Skt.): Literally, "action." The Buddhist teaching that all our actions have consequences that carry into the future. As sentient beings we experience consequences from actions performed in previous lives. Similarly, our actions in our current life lay the foundation for consequences in a future life. It should be noted that it is not the self [since there is no "self"] that transmigrates from one life to the next, but the karmic store of conditions, which can mature into consequences in a future life.

*kleshas* (Skt.): Literally "poisons or defilements." Sometimes translated as vexations or afflictions. Kleshas are attributes of mind that lead to unwholesome actions and attachments. Among the pervasive kleshas are desire, anger, and delusion.

*Lam Rim* (Tib.): A systematic presentation of the path to enlightenment in Tibetan Buddhism that begins from commitment to a teacher to the higher learnings of shamata and vipashyana. The most famous one is perhaps the *Lam Rim Chen Mo*, or the *Great Stages of the Path*, by Lama Tsongkhapa (1357-1419).

*Lankavatara Sutra* (Skt.): A scripture propounding various Mahayana theories, such as eight consciousnesses and tathagatagarbha or buddha-nature. It also served as a scriptural basis for the Indian Yogachara School. See eight consciousnesses.

Linji (Jap. Rinzai): One of the two great schools of Chan Buddhism, the other being the Caodong (Jap. Soto) School. This school is named after its founder, Master Linji, who sometimes used startling methods, such as shouting and beating, to bring his students to awakening.

*Lotus Sutra* or the *Saddharmapandarika Sutra* (Skt.): A Mahayana scripture known for its concept of the unification of the different vehicles of Buddhism and for its extensive instruction on the use of "expedient means," mostly in the form of parables.

Madhyamika (Skt.): A major school of Mahayana philosophy that expounds the truth of causes and conditions and emptiness, founded by the Indian saint Nagarjuna (circa 2nd-3rd century CE). The teachings of Madhyamika were transmitted to China as the Three-Treatise (Chn. Sanlun) School through texts such as the *Treatise of the Middle Way*, or *Madhyamikakarika*.

*mahamudra* (Skt.): A special practice of the Kagyu school of Tibetan Buddhism, in which one trains to directly experience the empty and luminous nature of mind.

*Commentary on the Sutra of the Great Transcendent Wisdom* or *Mahaprajnaparamita Sastra*: A commentary in 100 fascicles, on the *Mahaprajnaparamiṭa Sutra*, or the *Scripture of Great Transcendent Wisdom*, attributed to Nargarjuna.

Mahayana (Skt.): Literally, "Great Vehicle," the Buddhist path of the bodhisattva contrasted to the Hinayana path of personal liberation. See Bodhisattva, Hinayana.

Maitreya (Skt.): The future Buddha who is believed to now dwell in the Tushita Heaven, awaiting his next incarnation.

Nyingmapa (Tib.): One of the four main schools of Tibetan Buddhism, the others being the Sakyapa, Kagyupa, and Gelugpa.

nirvana (Skt.): Literally, "extinction." State of ultimate liberation in which one is liberated from vexations [Skt. kleshas], suffering, and the cycle of birth and death. In the Hinayana, nirvana is defined as a state free from rebirth; in the Mahayana, nirvana attained by bodhisattvas is sometimes conceived as a liberation within the cycle of birth and death—a nirvana without a specific location.

*paramitas* (Skt.): Literally, "perfections," often referred to as the Six Paramitas, practices followed in fulfillment of the bodhisattva path and consisting of generosity (Skt. *dana*), discipline (Skt. *shila*), patience (Skt. *kshanti*), effort (Skt. *virya*), meditation (Skt. dhyana), and wisdom (Skt. prajna).

*Platform Sutra*: Although called a "sutra," this text is really a record of the sayings and doings of Huineng (638-713 CE) the Sixth Patriarch of Chan. The text emphasizes sudden enlightenment, the inseparability of samadhi and prajna, and other key concepts that contributed to the formation of the Chan tradition, as well as formlessness, non-thought, and non-abiding.

prajna (Skt.): Literally, "wisdom." In Buddhism, prajna is a fundamental quality, along with compassion, of enlightened mind. In terms of Buddhist realization, prajna is the directly perceived insight into phenomena as "empty."

Sakyapa (Tib.): One of the four main schools of Tibetan Buddhism, the others being the Kagyupa, Nyingmapa, and Gelugpa.

samadhi (Skt.): State of deep meditative absorption characterized by a focused awareness of the mind itself. In traditional Buddhist understanding, samadhi is related to prajna but not identical with it. In Chan, samadhi and prajna are inseparable.

samsara (Skt.): The cycle of birth and death that sentient beings experience, until they achieve ultimate enlightenment, nirvana. See nirvana.

sentient being: Any being who possesses a mind that is contaminated by delusion (Skt. Avidya) and other vexations (Skt. kleshas). It is a term used to distinguish an ordinary person from a buddha. On a noumenon level, a sentient being is equal to a buddha. However, on a phenomenon level, a budha cannot really be refered to as an ordinary sentient being.

shamata (Skt.): Meditative practice that focuses on stilling the mind in order to reach meditative equipoise, often associated with vipashyana or "insight" meditation that gives rise to the wisdom of emptiness. The Tiantai School is noted for its teachings on shamata and vipashyana meditation in both the "gradual and progressive" and "perfect and sudden" approaches.

*shastra* (Skt.): Treatise written by followers of Buddhism, usually being a commentary on one of the sutras, or a synthesis of Buddhist concepts. See sutra.

shunyata (Skt.): Literally, "emptiness or void," the experience of the fundamental emptiness of phenomena, including the "self." Shunyata is therefore considered the experience of one's own buddha-nature.

stupa: a pagoda-like building that contains sacred relics of Buddha or great practitioners.

sutra (Skt.): Buddhist scripture, as expounded by the Shakyamuni Buddha during forty-five years of teaching following his own enlightenment. Originally transmitted orally, the sutras were not written until several centuries after the Buddha's nirvana. See shastra.

Tantrayana (Skt.): The esoteric and yogic path in Tibetan Buddhism, with emphasis on meditation, visualization, and the study of tantric texts. Tantrayana primarily teaches the path to awakening through purification and transformation. Synonymous with Vajrayana and Mantrayana.

*tathagatagarbha* (Skt.): The supreme Buddha principle, indwelling in all sentient beings, providing the potential ground to become enlightened.

*Ten Stages of the Bodhisattva Scripture* or the *Dasabhumika Sutra* (Skt.): A scripture that explains the ten stages of the bodhisattva path.

In Chinese Buddhism, this scripture is absorbed into the larger version of the *Avatamsaka Sutra.*

*tetralemma* (Skt.): Nagarjuna's fourfold method of analyzing reality through 1) affirmation, 2) negation, 3) both affirmation and negation, 4) neither affirmation nor negation. Nagarjuna shows how all propositions are ultimately unable to describe reality. Therefore, all propositions or conceptions of reality are false.

Tiantai School: a Chinese Mahayana school, based on the *Lotus Sutra*, established by Great Master Zhiyi (538-597). The hallmark of the school is its development and delineation of the systems of calming and insight meditations. See shamata and vipashyana.

*Treasure of Manifest Knowledge* or the *Abhidharmakoshabhashyam* (Skt.): Treatise by Vasubandhu (400-480 CE) summarizing the doctrines of Hinayana. This text includes detailed analysis of human consciousness in its relationship to the environment, as well as the transformations that occur in meditation practice.

Tri-song-Deutsen (Tib.): Tibetan king under whose reign Buddhism spread with great zeal after he had invited the Abbot Shantarakshita and Acharya Padmasambhava to Tibet and the Buddha's teachings were translated.

Tsongkhapa (1357-1419): Lama (teacher) and founder of the Gelugpa or Ganden School of Tibetan Buddhism that based its doctrines on the Kadampa school of Tibet established by the great Indian master Atisha (982-1054).

twelve links of dependent origination: In Buddhism, the twelve stages in the cycle of birth and death, beginning with delusion arising from karmic conditions, ending with death, and starting the cycle again. See delusion.

*Vajrayana* (Skt.): See Tantrayana.

*Vimalakirtinirdesha Sutra* (Skt.): Major scripture that expounds the profound principle of Mahayana and refutes the Hinayana view through the protagonist, the layman Bodhisattva Vimalakirti.

Vinaya School: School of Buddhist studies, especially active in the early period of transmission of Buddhism in China, specializing in researching and interpreting the Buddhist codes of discipline called vinaya.

*Vipashyana* (Skt.): Insight meditation. *Lhagthong* in Tibetan. See shamata.

Yogachara (Skt.): See Consciousness-Only School.

DHARMA DRUM PUBLICATIONS

Dharma Drum Publications is a nonprofit publisher of books, CDs, videos, and cassettes on Buddhism and Chan [Zen].

All of our materials promote understanding of Buddhism as a living philosophy with a commitment to preserve and transmit important works from the Buddhist tradition.

Dharma Drum Publications is located at the Chan Meditation Center in New York and is part of the International Cultural and Educational Foundation of Dharma Drum Mountain [DDM] in Taiwan, founded in 1989 by Venerable Master Sheng-yen. The foundation includes a Buddhist Institute, monasteries, retreat centers, communities, and publishing houses. DDM offers programs that focus on the spiritual and educational needs of people at all stages of their lives. Some of these programs include international Buddhist conferences, ecological seminars and lectures, social welfare programs, and meditation retreats.

For information about Venerable Master Sheng-yen and his retreat community in the United States and Taiwan, please contact:


Chan Meditation Center
90-56 Corona Avenue
Elmhurst, New York 11373 USA
Tel: 718/592-6593 Fax: 718/592-0717
Email: ddmbany@aol.com

Dharma Drum Retreat Center
184 Quannacut Road
Pine Bush, NY 12566 USA
Tel: 914/744-8114 Fax: 914/744-8483

Nung Chan Monastery
89, Lane 65, Ta Ye Road
Peitou 11242
Taipei, Taiwan R.O.C.
Tel: 2893-2783, 2894-8811 Fax: 22896-7780
Email: gguangs@ddm.org.tw

## BOOKS IN ENGLISH BY VENERABLE MASTER SHENG-YEN

*Getting the Buddha Mind*
*The Poetry of Enlightenment–Poems by Ancient Chan Masters*
*Faith in Mind*
*Infinite Mirror*
*The Sword of Wisdom*
*Dharma Drum: The Life and Heart of Chan Practice*
*Complete Enlightenment*

## FORTHCOMING BOOKS

*Hoofprint of the Ox*
*Illuminating Silence: The Practice of Silent Illumination*

If you would like to subscribe to our free Chan Magazine or receive other free books, please contact:


Dharma Drum Publications
90-56 Corona Avenue
Elmhurst, New York 11373 USA

Tel: 718/595-0915 Fax: 718-592-0717
Email: dharmadrm@aol.com
URL: http://www.chan1.org